A Summary of What Happened by Hillary Rodham Clinton:

What Hillary Meant to Say

By Grady Paul

I
Shared
My
Tax
Return

F*cking

Heat

Exhaustion

Comey

Has

Really

Bad

Timing

The
Whole
Sex
Cult
Thing

Those

Damn

White

People

Those
Damn
Men

Those

Damn

Racists

I
Didn't
Let
Bill
Sleep
With
Putin

I'm
As
Interesting
As
A
Wet
Carrot

Melania

Is

Better

Looking

Than

Bill

Free

Will

I

Let

Bill

Sling

Dick

All

Over

Town

I'm
Corrupt
And
Don't
Even
Hide
It

The

DNC

Ole

Bernie

I

Think

Country

Folks

Are

Morans

Kung

Fu

Pander

Trumps

Twitter

Fingers

Cold

Lifeless

Eyes

Pepe

The

Frog

Obamacare

Sleazebag Anthony Weiner

The

Deplorables

I'm

A

Career

Politician

I
Failed
The
DC
Bar
Exam

Not Enough Donors

Fake

News

Fox

News

Clinton Foundation

WikiLeaks

Ghost Of Seth Rich

#spiritcooking

#MAGA

#HillarysHealth

Doughboy

Tim

Kaine

Wall

Street

$peeche$

James

O'Keefe

Angela Merkel

CNN

Rigged

The

Debate

Mike Cernovich

Lil'

Ben

Shapiro

www.reddit.com/The Donald

Benghazi

Libya

Syria

Alex

Jones

"Superpredators"

Lied

So

Much

My

Pants

Are

On

Fire

I

Couldn't

Even

Win

A

Rigged

Election

Keith Olberman

If
Only
Chachi
Supported
Me

That

Fly

That

Parked

On

My

Face

Vegans

Millennials Don't Vote

Donald

Mother

F*cking

TRUMP

Made in the USA
Columbia, SC
05 December 2017